THREE

MW01602133

THREE WORKS ON ALCHEMY

THE IMMORTAL LIQUOR ALKAHEST

EVERBURNING LIGHTS

THE PHILOSOPHIC FIRE

ALKAHEST, 1683
EIRENAEUS PHILALETHES

EVERBURNING LIGHTS, 16th CENTURY
JOHANNES TRITHEMIUS

PHILOSOPHIC FIRE, 16th CENTURY
JOHN PONTANUS

NEW EDITION 2016
EDITED BY TARL WARWICK

COPYRIGHT AND DISCLAIMER

FOREWORD

Herein are three works which are too short on their own account to ever release singularly, all three of which form important parts of alchemy.

First then there is the Immortal Liquor, Alkahest-this material is used in the processing of alchemical elixir and used during the process of making the stone of the philosophers. Through this text, written by Philalethes in the late 1600s, in the form of questions and answers, the student of alchemy is supposedly able to understand both what the Alkahest is and how it is produced.

Secondly the interesting tract on everburning lights created by Trithemius. This little manuscript is told partly in recipe form and partly as a short back story by which the working of Trithemius is referred to in the past tense. It is said here that through a relatively simplistic process, a glowing, apparently phosphorescent reaction of extremely long duration can be produced using relatively mundane materials and a furnace, and that the resulting glowing lights at one time were purchased by the emperor Maximillian at great expense and were plural in manufacture.

The third text here is a reference to the fire of the philosophers, specifically the same fire referred to in every other alchemical work. Pontanus here refutes Geber and many others and speaks of their works being too confusing on the subject to be useful at all until a person becomes aware of the exact nature of the philosophic fire required to create the stone of the philosophers within alchemy. He then alludes to Artephius and points to his writings as the key to the mystery (a likely allusion specifically to the Secret Book of Artephius) which speaks of the secret fire.

THE IMMORTAL LIQUOR
ALKAHEST

Q. What is the Alkahest?

A. It is a Catholic and universal menstruate, and, in a word, may be called Ignis Aqua, a Fiery-Water, an uncompounded and immortal ens, which is penetrative, resolving all things unto their first liquid matter, nor can anything resist its power, for it acts without any reaction from the patient: nor does it suffer from anything but its equal by which it is brought into subjection; but after it has dissolved all other things it remains entire in its former nature, and is of the same virtue after a thousand operations as at the first.

Q. Of what substance is it?

A. It is a noble circulated salt, prepared with wonderful art till it answers the desires of an ingenious artist, yet is it not any corporeal salt made liquid by a bare solution, but is a saline spirit which heat cannot coagulate by evaporation of the moisture but is of a spiritual uniform substance, volatile with a gentle heat, leaving nothing behind it, yet is not this spirit either acidic or alkaline but salt.

Q. What is its equal?

A. If you know the one, you may without difficulty know the other: Seek therefore for the gods have made arts the reward of industry.

Q. What is the next matter of the Alkahest?

A. I have told you that it is a salt, the fire surrounded the salt and the water swallowed up the fire, yet overcame it not, so is made the philosophers' fire, of which they speak; "The vulgar burn with fire, we with water."

Q. What is the most noble salt?

A. If you desire to learn this descend into yourself, for you carry it about with you, as well the salt, as its extractor, if you are able to discern it.

Q. Which is it, tell me I pray you?

A. Man's blood out of the body, or man's Lotium, for the urine is an excrement separated for the greatest part from the blood. Each of these give both a volatile and fixed salt, if you know how to collect and prepare it you will have a most precious balm of life.

Q. Is the property of human urine nobler than the urine of any beast?

A. By many degrees, for though it be an excrement only, yet its salt has not its like in the whole universal nature.

Q. What are its parts?

A. One volatile and one more fixed; yet according to the variety of ordering it, these may be variously altered.

Q. Are there any things in urine which are different from its inmost specific urinaceous nature?

A. There are; namely, a watery phlegm, and sea salt which we take in with our meat, and remains entire and undigested in the urine, and by separation may be divided from it, which (if there be no sufficient use of it in the meat after a convenient time) ceases.

Q. Whence is that phlegm or insipid watery salt?

A. It is chiefly from our several drinks, and yet everything hath its own phlegm.

Q. Explain yourself more clearly?

A. You must know that the urine partly by the separative virtue, is conveyed with what we drink to the bladder; partly consists of a watery teffas (an excremental humor of the blood) whence being separated by the odor of the urinaceous ferment it penetrates most deeply, the saltiness being unchanged, unless that the saltiness of the blood and urine be both the same; so that whatsoever is contained in the urine besides salt is unprofitable phlegm.

Q. How does it appear that there is a plentiful phlegm in urine?

A. Thus suppose, first from the taste, secondly from the weight, thirdly from the virtue of it.

Q. Be your own Mercurius?

A. The salt of urine contains all that is properly essential to the urine, the smell whereof is very sharp, the taste differs according as it is differently ordered, so that sometimes it is also salt with an urinaceous saltiness.

Q. What have you observed concerning the weight thereof?

A. I have observed thus much; that three ounces or a little more of urine taken from a healthy man, will moderately out weigh about eighty grains of Fountain Water, from whence also I have seen a liquor distilled which was of equal weight to the said water, whence it is evident that most of the salt was left behind.

Q. What have you observed of its virtue?

A. The congealing of urine by cold is an argument that phlegm is in it; for the salt of urine is not so congealed if a little moistened with a liquid, though it be water.

Q. But this same phlegm though most accurately separated by distillation, retains the nature of urine, as may be perceived both by the smell and taste?

A. I confess it, though little can be discerned by taste, nor can you perceive more either by smell or taste, than you may from salt of urine dissolved in pure water.

Q. What doth Pyrotechny teach you concerning urine?

A. It teaches this, to make the salt of urine volatile.

Q. What is then left?

A. The earthly blackish stinking dregs.

Q. Is the spirit wholly uniform?

A. So it appears to the sight, smell and taste; and yet contains qualities directly contrary to each other.

Q. Which are they?

A. By one through its innate virtue the material is coagulated, by the other it is dissolved.

Q. What further?

A. In the coagulation of urine its spirit of wine is discovered.

Q. Is there such a spirit in urine?

A. There is indeed, truly residing in every urine, even of the most healthful man most which may be prepared by art.

Q. Of what efficacy is this spirit?

A. Of such as is to be lamented, and indeed may move our pity to mankind.

Q. Why so?

A. From hence the material has his own fierce enemy.

Q. Will you give an example of this thing?

A. I will. Take urine and dissolve in it a convenient quantity of saltpeter: Let it stand a month, afterwards distill it, and there will come over a spirit which burns upon the tongue like a coal of fire, pour this spirit on again and re-distill it four or five times, abstracting every time not above half, so the spirit becomes most piercing, yet not in the least sharp; the heat which goes out in the first distillation of the liquor, afterwards grows sensibly mild, and at length almost (if not altogether) vanishes, and the second spirit may be perceived mild both by the smell and taste which, in the former was most sharp.

Q. What have you observed concerning the former spirit?

A. If it be a little shaken, oily streaks appear sliding here and there, just as spirit of wine distills down the head of the alembic in streaks like veins.

Q. What kind of putrefaction should the urine

undergo that such a spirit may be had from it?

A. In a heat scarce to be perceived by sense; in a vessel lightly closed or covered rather; it may also be sometimes hotter sometimes cooler, so that neither the heat nor cold exceed a due mean.

Q. How may this winy spirit become most perspicuous?

A. By such a putrefaction which causes a ferment, and excites ebullition, (which will not happen in a long time) if the urine be kept in a wooden vessel, and in a place which is not hot (but yet keeps out the cold) as suppose behind a furnace in winter, where let it be kept till of itself a ferment arise in the urine and stirs up bubbles, for then you may draw from it a burning water which is somewhat like wine.

Q. Is there any other spirit of urine?

A. There is; for urine putrefied with a gentle heat the space of a fortnight or thereabout sends forth a coagulating spirit which will coagulate well rectified *Aqua Vitae.*

Q. How is that spirit to be prepared which forms the

counterpart of itself with a clear watery stalagma; and also that which dissolves the same?

A. Lotium putrefied for a month and half in a separate heat (most like the heat of horses' dung) will give you in a fit vessel successive stalagma according to your desire.

Q. Does every spirit of urine coagulate the spirit of wine?

A. By no means; this second spirit observed to lack that virtue.

Q. What does urine thus ordered contain besides the aforesaid spirits?

A. It contains more fixed urinaceous salt and by accident foreign marine salt.

Q. Can this more fixed salt be brought over the alembic with a gentle heat in form of a liquor?

A. It may, but art and ingenuity are required.

Q. Where is the phlegm?

A. In the salt; for in the preparation of putrefaction the salt being putrefied in the phlegm ascends together with it.

Q. Can it be separated?

A. It may, but not by every artist.

Q. What will this spirit do, when it is brought to this?

A. Try and you will wonder at what you shall see in the solution of bodies.

Q. Is not this the Alkhest?

A. This liquor cannot consist without partaking of the virtues of man's blood and in urine the footsteps thereof are observable.

Q. In urine therefore and blood the Alkahest lies hid?

A. Nature gives us both blood and urine; and from the nature of these Pyrotechny gives us a salt which art circulates into the circulated salt of Paracelsus.

Q. You speak short?

A. I will add this; the salt of blood ought so to be transmuted by the urinaceous ferment that it may lose its last life preserve its middle life, and retain its saltiness.

Q. To what purpose is this?

A. To manifest the excellency which is in man's blood above all other blood whatever, which is to be communicated to the urine (after an excremental liquor is separated from it) whence this urine excels as others in a wonderful virtue.

Q. Why do you add urine?

A. You must know that to transmute things a corrupting ferment is required, in which respect all other salts give place to the strong urinaceous salt.

Q. Cannot the phlegm be collected apart from the salt?

A. It may, if the urine be not first putrefied.

Q. How great a part of the water is to be reckoned phlegm?

A. Nine parts of ten or there about distilled from fresh urine are to be rejected, the tenth part (as much as can be extracted in form of liquor) is to be kept; from that dried urine which remains in the bottom by a gentle fire (which will not cause sublimation) let the salt be extracted with water, so that there be as much water as of that urine whence this feces was dried whatsoever is imbibed by the water. Let it poured off by decanting, let it be strained or purged *per deliquium*, then filter it through a glass: Let fresh water be poured on, and reiterate this work till the salt become pure then join this vastly stinking salt with your last spirit and distill it many times.

Praised be the name of the Lord... Amen.

THE EVERBURNING LIGHTS OF TRITHEMIUS

TWO ETERNAL UNQUENCHABLE BURNING TEMPORAL LIGHTS

Two unquenchable eternal lights are found and to be seen herein, which I Bartholomeus Korndorffer have written of a disciple of Mr. Trithemius, Abbot of Sponheim, which did affirm with an oath that they were never published nor opened before, only the Abbot had bestowed one of them unto a great potentate. This famous man, Trithemius, lived in time of the great emperor Maximilian the first, and none like unto him was to be found in his age, he had done much good with his arts, not mingled with Devilish works, as some malicious men do accuse him, but he did know anything he wished to know that was done in the world, by the stars of ministry, and he had also told of things to come many times.

Once as I was traveling, I came to St. Moritz, and found an acquaintance to whom I spoke, he was glad to see me, he invited me to dinner, and another named Servatius Hohel, which had been with the Abbot at Sponheim and served him twelve years. He was very civil, and at a few times he spoke a word of this art.

Now as we came together, and dinner being passed, Mr. Hohell desired me to go with him to his chamber, which i did discoursing of diverse matter of arts and, seeing he was an ancient man, I desired to leave him alone to his study but he would not give me leave, and bespoke a meal by his hostess, which we two did take in his chamber. Mr. Hohel did bestow upon me at that time, the handwriting of Mr Trithemius wherein these two incombustible lights were written, and some magick pieces, which I did try to prove afterwards and found them to be very true and right.

Mr. Hohel told me also that his Mr. Trithemius had bestowed one of those lights unto this great potentate, the emperor Maximilian, and placed it in a glass in his chamber, which the said potentate had kept very well, and many had seen the lightning thereof. After that a sickness arose and the emperor did depart from that place, and came not to this place again in twenty years, but as he came back once more at last, Mr. Trithemius beiing dead long before, he remembered this light and went presently to see it, which was found there with all tokens unquenchable as Mr. Trithemius had left it, and the people of that castle told the emperor that they had seen continually a lightning in that place, like a lamp in a church. Wherefore this emperor left the light years still burning where it shall shine still at this day, which is a great secret in this world. the emperor Maximilian has given 6000 crowns for those temporal everlasting lights.

PROCESS AND PRACTICE

Take four ounces of sulfur, and so much of calcined alum, grind them together, put it into an earthen sublimatory, place it into a coal fire, well lighted, let the sulfur ascend through the alum, and in eight hours is it prepared.

Of this material take at least 2 1/2 ounces, and one ounce of good crystalline Venetian porras [1], crush and powder these finely together, put it into a flat glass that it may lie flatly.

Pour upon it a strong, sharp, 4 times distilled spirit of wine and extract it in ashes softly to gain an oil, then pour it upon again, extract it to the oil again, pour it upon again and draw it off again.

Take a little of the sulfur, lay it upon a red hot copper plate, and when it flows like wax without smoking then is it prepared, if not then must you extract thereof more of the spirit of wine, till it sustains the proof, and it shall now be prepared.

Now take alumephume [2], make thereof a top not as long as a little finger, and half as thick, fold it about with white silk, put it thus whole into a Venetian little glass, and join thereunto of the prepared sulfur, place it a day and night in hot sand, that the top be continually in the sulfur.

Now take the top there-out, and put it into such a glass, that the top looks out a little. Add thereunto of the prepared incombustible material, place the glass into hot sand till the sulfur melts, and cleaves beneath and upward about the top, that it be seen but a little above, kindle the top with a common light, and it begins to burn presently, and the sulfur remains flowing. Take the light and place it where you wish, and it burns continually forever.

NOTES

1. Possibly volcanic glass.
2. Possibly aluminum.

THE PHILOSOPHIC FIRE

I, John Pontanus, who have traveled into various realms and domains on my quest to know of a certainty what is the philosophers' stone, journeying through all parts of the world, found but false philosophers and deceivers. Studying still, none the less, in the books of the wise, and my doubts increasing, I discovered the truth: And yet, notwithstanding I had knowledge of the material, I erred two hundred times before finding the operation and practice of that true material.

I commenced first my operations with putrefaction of the body of this material over a period of nine months but this came to naught. I placed it in the bain-made for lengthy periods, erring just the same. I took and placed it in the calcinating fire for three months and proceeded awry. All sorts and kinds of distillation and sublimation spoken of, or apparently spoken of by the philosophers- Geber, Archelaus, and almost any other- have I attempted and tried, and found equally nothing. In brief, I tried to come at and perfect in every way conceivable the subject of all the art of alchemy, be this by manure, bathing, ashes, or the thousand other sorts of fife mentioned by the philosophers in their works, but nothing did I discover of worth.

It was for this reason that I set myself to study the books of the philosophers for three years continually, studying among others those of Hermes, whose brief words contain the whole magistery of the stone; though he speaks quite obscurely of things above and below, of heaven and of the earth.

All one's application and care must then be only to know the correct practice in the first, second and third works. It is not at all the fire of the bath, dung or ashes, nor any of the other fires of which the philosophers sing or describe for us in their books.

What, then is this fire which perfects and achieves the entire work, from beginning to end? Certainly all philosophers have hidden it; but for myself, touched by a moment of pity, I would declare it and the achievement of the whole work.

The philosophers' stone is unique, and one, but hidden and veiled in a multiplicity of different names, and before knowing it you will have seen much struggle: Only with difficulty will you come to know it by your own genius. It is watery, airy, fiery and earthy, phlegmatic, choleric, sanguine and melancholy. It is a sulfur and equally mercury.

It has several types of superfluity which I assure you by the living God, transform themselves into one unique essence, if only there be our fire. And whoever believing such to be necessary would subtract anything from the subject, knows of a certainty nothing of philosophy. For the superfluous, unclean, foul, scurvy, miry and, in general, entire substance of the subject, is perfected into one fixed spiritual body, by means of our fire. Which has never been revealed by the wise, thus making it that but few succeed in this art; imagining that some foul and unworthy thing must be separated out.

Now must one make appear, and draw out the properties of our fire; if it agree with our material in the way of which I have spoken, that is to say, if it be transmuted with the material. This fire burns the material not at all, nor separates anything from it, nor divides nor puts apart the parts pure and impure, as is told by all philosophers, but converts the whole subject into purity. It does not sublime as Geber or Arnold and all others who have spoken of sublimation and distillation sublime. And it makes and perfects itself in little time.

This fire is mineral, equal and continual, and never evaporates unless over-excited; it has certain of the characteristics of sulfur, is taken and originates elsewhere than in the material. It ruptures, dissolves, and congeals all things, and similarly congeals and calcinates; it is difficult to find by industry or by art. This fire is the epitome and abridgment of the work in its entirety, taking no other thing else, or very little, and this same fire introduces itself and is of mediocre heat; for with this little fire the whole work is perfect, and all due and necessary sublimation achieved together.

Those who read Geber and all other philosophers shall never come to an understanding of it though they live one hundred million years; for this fire may not be discovered but by the sole and profound meditation of the mind, following which one will understand the books, and not otherwise. Error in this art, consists only in the acquisition of this fire, which converts the material into the stone of the wise.

Study, then, this fire, for had I myself found it at the first, I should not have erred two hundred times upon the veritable material. By which am I no longer surprised if so many come not to the accomplishment of the work. They err, have erred and will ever err, in that the philosophers have placed their veritable agent in but one, single thing, which Artephius named, but speaking only for himself. Had I not read Artephius, nor penetrated and understood, never would I have arrived at the accomplishment of the work.

Here, then, the practice: take the material with all diligence, grind and pulverize it physically and place it in the fire, that is within the oven; but the degree and proportion of the fire must also be known. To wit, that the external fire excite only the material; and in a little time this fire, without that one put a hand to it in any manner, will assuredly realize the work in its entirety. For it will purify, corrupt, engender and bring to perfection the whole work, making appear the three principal colors, the black, white and red. And by our fire the medicine will multiply, not only in quantity but also in virtue, if joined with the material in its raw state.

Search, therefore, this fire with all strength of your mind, and you shall reach the goal you have set yourself; for it is this that brings to completion all the stages of the work, and is the key of all the philosophers, which they have never revealed in their books. If you think well and deep upon this above-mentioned fire, you will know it. Not otherwise.

Thus, moved by a moment of pity, I have written this; but, and that I satisfy myself, as I made mention above, the fire is in no wise transmuted with the material. I wished to speak this and to warn well the prudent concerning these things, that they spend not in vain their money, but know in advance what it is that they seek and, by this means, arrive at the truth of the art; not otherwise. God keep thee.